START TO FOLLOW
Seven Lessons on the Basics of the Christian Faith

Text Copyright © 2020, 2011, 2006, 2005 by Harvest Ministries. All rights reserved.

Design and Typesetting: Harvest Design
Copywriting: Leah Case
Copyediting: Harvest Publications

Unless otherwise noted, Scripture quotations are from the Holy Bible, New Living Translation. Copyright ©1996, 2004, 2015 by Tyndale House Foundation. Used by permission of Tyndale House Publishers, Inc., Carol Stream, Illinois 60188. All rights reserved.

Scripture quotations marked NKJV are taken from the New King James Version®. Copyright © 1982 by Thomas Nelson. Used by permission. All rights reserved.

Scripture quotations marked NIV are taken from the Holy Bible, New International Version® NIV®. Copyright © 1973, 1978, 1984, 2011 by Biblica, Inc.™. Used by permission of Zondervan. All rights reserved worldwide. www.zondervan.com. The "NIV" and "New International Version" are trademarks registered in the United States Patent and Trademark Office by Biblica, Inc.™

Scripture quotations marked NASB are taken from the New American Standard Bible® (NASB), Copyright © 1960, 1962, 1963, 1968, 1971, 1972, 1973, 1975, 1977, 1995 by The Lockman Foundation. Used by permission. www.Lockman.org

All rights reserved under international copyright conventions. No part of this booklet may be reproduced in any form or by any means, electronic or mechanical, including photocopying, recording, or by any information storage and retrieval system, without written permission from this publisher. Inquiries should be addressed to: Harvest Ministries, P.O. Box 4000, Riverside, California, 92514-4000.

Printed in the United States of America.

ISBN-13: 978-1-61754-012-7

Contents

Foreword by Greg Laurie		1
Introduction—Saved! Now What?		3
1	The Bible: Your User's Guide for Life *Study God's Word*	7
2	Why Is Church Important? *Fellowship and Service*	13
3	I've Never Done That Out Loud! *Worship and Prayer*	21
4	I Have Good News! *Sharing Your Faith*	27
5	Decisions, Decisions *Knowing and Doing God's Will*	35
6	Growing Pains *Trials and Temptations*	43
7	Trinity 101 *A Beginner's Guide to God's Nature*	49
Developing Your Personal Quiet Time		56

Foreword

"If you want to accept Jesus Christ, get up right now and walk forward." The next thing I knew, I was getting up and walking over. I stood in a little huddle of people, and we prayed. Then the school bell rang.

I made a commitment to Christ that day in high school, and I have stood by that commitment. I wasn't raised in the church. I wasn't biblically literate. But I wanted to know God. I wanted to know the meaning of life. I wanted to grow and live like Christ.

I'm very thankful for those believers who came alongside me in my early days as a Christian and helped me get started on the right foot. They modeled, taught, and helped me understand what it meant to follow Christ. I didn't know it at the time, but I was being discipled.

Not every person who comes to faith in Christ will have someone to disciple them or will know where to find resources or ministries that can help them grow spiritually. Their first days and months as a Christian will be more difficult.

That's why it is critical to equip both new and mature believers with biblical teaching and helpful resources that will encourage them to grow in their relationship with Christ and to share their faith with others.

Because both new and mature Christians can have trouble knowing just what it means to follow Christ, we've developed a resource called *Start to Follow: Seven Lessons on the Basics of the Christian Faith*. This how-to manual explains essentials like Bible study, prayer, fellowship, and sharing your faith.

It will not take the place of having a caring group of Christians, like I had, to disciple you. But it will guide you, and it can be a great resource to fill in the gaps of your Christian walk. Through interactive, workbook-style questions, you will learn the key biblical principles and Scripture that every believer should know.

I believe this is a valuable resource for every Christian—for brushing up on the basics, as well as for sharing with someone who is younger or brand-new in the faith.

You might find that you have some gaps in your knowledge of what it really means to follow Christ. *Start to Follow* can help you and anyone in your family or circle of friends to become more solidly grounded in their faith. Then you can pass it on to a new Christian!

We all have a part to play. Just as God used that group of Christians on my high school campus to get my attention and point me toward Christ, I believe that He wants to use each one of us in the lives of those who don't yet know Him. Thank you for being willing.

Greg Laurie
Senior Pastor
Harvest Christian Fellowship

INTRODUCTION
Saved! *Now What?*

Welcome to God's family! You have made the most important decision of your life, choosing to follow Jesus. As a new believer, you have questions. You prayed and asked Jesus into your heart, but now you want to know what that actually means.

First, you need to know that means you are headed in the right direction—you are bound for Heaven. Before coming to Christ, you were separated from God by sin and on your way to a very real place called Hell! But Jesus has saved you by dying on the cross in your place. The Bible says:

Since we have been made right in God's sight by the blood of Christ, he will certainly save us from God's condemnation. For since our friendship with God was restored by the death of his Son while we were still his enemies, we will certainly be saved through the life of his Son. (Romans 5:9–10)

Second, you need to know that you have been given a new life! The Bible says, that "anyone who belongs to Christ has become a new person. The old life is gone; a new life has begun!" (2 Corinthians 5:17).

As a new believer, you can expect to have new attitudes and desires. You may need to replace some old habits and patterns with new activities that will help you to grow your new life in Christ. Growth takes time, but it begins—right now—where you are. Here is what you need to know in order to get off on the right foot:

READ THE BIBLE
The Bible will tell you everything you need to know in order to grow in your spiritual life. Because God speaks through His Word, you will get to know Him better and learn what pleases Him. As you obey His Word, you will grow strong and begin to see positive changes in your life.

PRAY
Prayer is one of the greatest privileges we have as a child of God. Just think, the God of all creation wants to hear from you! You can call on the Lord any hour of the day or night and He will listen. It doesn't matter to God if your prayers are eloquent or flowery—it matters only that you pray with a pure and sincere heart.

FIND A CHURCH TO ATTEND
Church plays a vital role in your spiritual growth. Fellowship with other Christians will keep you spiritually active and give you much needed encouragement and support. Church provides you with instruction from God's Word and gives you the training and opportunity to use your God-given gifts and abilities.

START LIVING FOR GOD
A sure sign of a changed heart is the desire to live for God. What does this mean? It means that you want to please God and to obey Him as best you know how. You will begin to filter your thoughts and actions through God's Word in order to become a reflection of Jesus Christ.

SHARE YOUR FAITH
Good news is hard to keep to yourself! God wants you to share your newfound faith with others. You don't have to wait until you're an expert in the Bible to witness to others. You can share what you know—your own story of what Jesus has done for you. See Chapter 4 for more on sharing your "One-Minute Message."

DON'T GET SIDETRACKED
Being a Christian is not always easy. There will be times when you'll feel pressured to back down or give in. When you became a child of God, you also became an enemy of the devil; and he will try to tempt you into disobeying God. It isn't a sin to be tempted—even Jesus experienced temptation (see Luke 4:1–3)—but giving in to the temptation is sin. Christians will experience times of testing and trials, but God promises to be with us and give us the strength we need to get through hard times.

This series is designed to help you take those first steps toward following Jesus. In each session, you will be asked to *read*, *reflect*, and *respond*.

READ
In this section, you will find what the Word of God has to say. Simple questions are designed to guide you and should be answered in your own words.

REFLECT
As you discover what God's Word says, you will want to take time to consider what this teaches you about God, about life, and about yourself.

RESPOND

Here is where the "rubber meets the road," so to speak. *What will you do with what you have learned?* Let your prayer be like the man who prayed, "Oh, that my actions would consistently reflect your decrees! As I learn your righteous regulations, I will thank you by living as I should!" (Psalm 119:5, 7).

To make your Bible study time more productive, here are a few suggestions and guidelines:

FIND A QUIET PLACE

Choose a time and place that will give you the best chance for concentration without distractions. It may be in your favorite chair, first thing in the morning, or in your car during the lunch break. If you're a night owl, that might be the best time for you. The "right" time and place is the one that works for you.

PLAN TO SPEND AT LEAST 30 MINUTES A DAY

Make a regular, daily appointment with God and commit to keeping it. This is *your* time to be alone with God for conversation, guidance, and strength for the day. Sadly, when Christians neglect this "quiet time," they miss out on what God has for them.

ALWAYS BEGIN WITH PRAYER

Ask God to help you understand what you read and to help you to have a teachable attitude.

BE READY AND WILLING TO CHANGE

Spiritual growth takes time and certainly no one ever became a spiritual giant overnight! But we stunt our own growth when we are unwilling to cooperate with the Holy Spirit, whom the Bible calls our Helper and Teacher (see John 14:26).

PRACTICE WHAT YOU LEARN

Jesus said, "Blessed [or happy] are all who hear the word of God and put it into practice" (Luke 11:28). What we learn by reading becomes truly ours when we put it into use. Determine to apply God's Word in your daily life and you will soon begin to see progress in your spiritual walk.

CHAPTER 1

The Bible: Your User's Guide for Life
STUDY GOD'S WORD

Babies are born hungry! Just as a tiny newborn instinctively craves mother's milk, so the spiritual newborn hungers for spiritual food. You can think of the Bible as food for your soul, providing the nourishment you need to grow in your relationship with the Lord. The Bible tells us: "You must crave pure spiritual milk so that you will grow into a full experience of salvation. Cry out for this nourishment, now that you have had a taste of the Lord's kindness" (1 Peter 2:2–3).

Another way you can think of the Bible is as your "User's Guide" for life. Like any good instruction manual, the Bible tells us how things fit together and what we need to do to keep our spiritual life in good working condition. Because God knows we need help, He has given us the Bible—complete with operating instructions, real-life illustrations, and warning labels. Everything we need to know, in order to live and grow, can be found in the pages of this God-inspired book.

In this session, you will begin to discover:

- The value of God's Word
- The benefits of God's Word
- The promises of God's Word

Before you start, be sure to pray. A simple prayer might go something like this:

Lord, I open my heart and mind to receive Your Word.
Please help me understand what I read in Your Word today.
Please teach me and help me to know how to apply what I learn.

READ

The Bible is unlike any other book you will ever read. What makes it so unique? It's a living book! The printed words on the page never change, but the Bible will always have something new and life-changing to show you. The author of Hebrews said it this way, "The word of God is alive and active. Sharper than any double-edged sword, it penetrates even to dividing soul and spirit, joints and marrow; it judges the thoughts and attitudes of the heart" (Hebrews 4:12 NIV).

You see, the Bible never stops speaking to humankind. It cuts across the surface of our words and actions and penetrates to the heart of the matter. It has been said that the heart of the matter is the matter of the heart. God's Word reveals all that is in our heart, good and bad. The Bible gives us insight into our own life—what is broken, what needs to change, and what absolutely must go. Only God's Word can pierce through sin's barrier and answer the need of every human heart.

Some people have the idea that the Bible is an outdated book filled with moral fables and endless lists of do's and don'ts. They don't believe the Bible is relevant for today. As you begin to study the Bible for yourself, you will discover the great value, benefit, and promises that are given to you, as a child of God, in the pages of this living book.

Let's take a look together.

- **Discover the Value of God's Word**

    The Bible is the only book you need in order to know God and walk with Him. It has stood the test of time and critical examination. What does the Bible say about itself? Read the verses given below and finish the sentence.

Psalm 12:6; Proverbs 30:5	God's Word is _____
Psalm 18:30	God's Word is _____
Psalm 119:160	God's Word is _____
Luke 21:33; 1 Peter 1:24–25	God's Word is _____

- **Discover the Benefit of God's Word**

  As you begin to walk in your new faith, you will find that God's Word proves true in your own life. In what ways can you expect to benefit from reading and obeying God's Word?

  Joshua 1:8 _____

  Psalm 119:11 _____

  Psalm 119:105, 130 _____

  Proverbs 2:9–11 _____

  2 Timothy 3:16–17 _____

- **Discover the Promises of God's Word**

  The Bible is full of God's promises to His children, which now includes you. Here are just a few to begin with. What do these verses say God has promised?

  Proverbs 8:17 _____

  Luke 11:9–10 _____

  John 10:27–29 _____

  John 14:23, 27 _____

REFLECT

In July 1999, the world was stunned by news that John F. Kennedy Jr. had perished in a plane crash, along with his wife and her sister. The son of the late president was piloting his private plane to Cape Cod, Massachusetts to attend a family wedding. Instead, his plane mysteriously plunged out of the night sky. Investigators found no mechanical problems with Kennedy's plane and concluded the probable cause was pilot error due to "spatial disorientation." The sky was covered by a blanket of haze that night, obscuring the horizon over the open water. While Kennedy had accumulated more than 300 hours of flight time, he was still working toward obtaining an instrument rating.

Typically, pilots in trouble are taught to ignore their physical senses and depend on their navigation equipment. Without the ability to fly solely by the instrument panel, a pilot can easily lose control of the aircraft, sometimes within seconds.

In life, we are faced with choices and decisions every day. The way is not always clear. We must decide whether to depend on our own instincts or look for guidance from a source outside ourselves. The Bible is the source of truth. God's Word is the "instrument panel" that will help us navigate safely through life.

If you will begin to follow three simple steps the Bible gives, you'll soon obtain an "instrument rating" in life—you won't be left to feel your way alone in the dark.

1. Pray for eyes to see. Read Psalm 119:18 and write it down here.

2. Pray for understanding. Read Psalm 119:27 and write it down here.

3. Pray for resolve to obey God's Word. Read Psalm 119:59–60 and write it down here.

Looking back over this session, what is the most important discovery you have made about God and His Word?

RESPOND

If you are convinced that it's important to get into God's Word so that God's Word can get into you—great! Now it's time to make a plan.

Make an appointment with God.
What time of day (or night) will I set aside to read and study the Bible?

The best place for me to do this is:

_____

_____

SCRIPTURE MEMORY

Your word I have hidden in my heart, that I might not sin against You.
—Psalm 119:11 NKJV

CHAPTER 2

Why Is Church Important?
FELLOWSHIP AND SERVICE

While personal Bible study is extremely important to your spiritual growth, you also need to make a regular practice of going to church. Why is church so important? For one thing, Jesus Himself established the church (see Matthew 16:18). The church is not just a building, but an assembly of people who believe (as Peter said in Matthew 16:16) that Jesus is the Christ, the Son of the living God.

In the New Testament, the words *temple* or *synagogue* are used to describe a building where people go to worship. The word *church* can be used to describe all genuine believers across the world—and throughout the ages. The church is also called "the body of Christ" (see Colossians 1:24). When you became a Christian, you became a part of the body of believers that is the church.

So why go to church? Because being involved in a local church is a vital part of growing your Christian faith. You need a place where you will be encouraged and instructed. You need a place where you can give out what God has given to you.

In this session, you will begin to discover:

- How the church will help you
- You have a place in the church
- The characteristics of a thriving church

Before you start, be sure to pray. A simple prayer might go something like this:

Lord, since You established the church, it must be important. Please help me to make a regular practice of going to church. Please show me how to get involved in my church in order to grow and to serve You.

READ

We need fellowship with other believers. This is something we never outgrow as Christians. Being part of a healthy church helps us to thrive and grow. As a new believer, you will find that being part of a local church is important for several reasons. Let's take a look together.

- **Discover How the Church Will Help You**

    The church will help you grow through the faithful teaching of God's Word. As a new believer, you are sure to have questions about what the Bible means. You are just beginning to discover the basics of the Christian faith. You need to be fed from God's Word and given spiritual instruction.

    In the previous chapter, you discovered the benefits of reading God's Word for yourself. The best way to establish and develop strong Bible study skills is by being part of a church where God's Word is opened and studied regularly.

    Why will a thriving church put great emphasis on Bible study? Read the verses below for the answer.

    2 Timothy 4:2-3 _____

    Ephesians 4:11-13 _____

A healthy, learning church is where the Spirit of God leads the people of God to submit to the Word of God.
—Greg Laurie

The church will help you grow through fellowship with other believers. We need to know that, as a member of God's family, we have a place to go for loving encouragement. In the church, we meet other people who share our love for Christ. Some believers have been faithfully walking with Christ for many years. You can learn from their example and gain wisdom for your own spiritual walk. In times of trial or tragedy, we need the comfort and support of Christians who will love us and stand with us.

Why is fellowship with other believers important? Read the verses below for the answer.

Hebrews 10:24–25 _____

Romans 1:11–12 _____

- **Discover Your Place in the Church**

  As you just read in Hebrews 10:24, believers are encouraged to "stir up love and good works" (NKJV) in one another. Church is a place to come to listen and learn—but it is also a place to serve. The fact is we need each other! Everyone has a role in the church.

  Serving others is one way of serving the Lord. As you look for opportunities to give out what you have received, you will find your place in the church.

  You may be wondering why the church would need you. Here are a few reasons to consider:

  Ephesians 2:10 _____

  Romans 12:4–5 _____

The church needs you! It needs your involvement, your gifts, your encouragement, your faith. So the next step is to find where God wants you.
—Greg Laurie

- **Characteristics of a Thriving Church**

    With so many churches to choose from, how do you go about finding the right one? The first thing to do, of course, is pray. Ask God to direct you to the place you can call your "church home." What does a thriving church look like? It will look a lot like the early church we read about in the New Testament.

    The story of the first church is found in Acts 2. After Peter spoke to a group of Jews that was gathered in Jerusalem for a festival, many believed and the church was born.

    These new believers were so committed to living for Christ and sharing the good news of Jesus Christ that they turned the world upside down (see Acts 17:6)! Looking at the New Testament church, we discover four characteristics of a thriving church—or a *W.E.L.L.* church. That is: ***worshipping, evangelizing, learning, and loving***.

    Read Acts 2:42 and write it down here:

    ___

    ___

    ## A WORSHIPPING CHURCH

    The early church was a place of worship and prayer. They made a regular practice of expressing their praise and faith in God. We will explore this more in the next session—for now, what did Jesus teach about worship? Read John 4:24 for the answer.

    ___

    ___

    ## AN EVANGELIZING CHURCH

    A worshipping church will also be a *growing* one. A growing church will consistently reach out to share the gospel. Having large attendance numbers is not a sign, by itself, of a spiritually thriving church. But a healthy church regularly evangelizes its community. What effect did the early church have in its community? Read Acts 2:41, 47 for the answer.

    ___

    ___

A LEARNING CHURCH

The apostles taught on the life and ministry of Jesus Christ. They weren't spreading their own ideas, but following the Lord's command. And the church matured spiritually, learning the word of God. What did Jesus tell the apostles to teach? Read Matthew 28:19–20 for the answer.

A LOVING CHURCH

The early believers devoted themselves to teaching and *fellowship*. In simple terms, this means they looked out for each other like a family. A thriving church overflows with love—for God, for each other, and for the lost. What did Jesus tell His disciples about love? Read John 13:34–35 for the answer.

REFLECT

There was a time when going to church on Sunday was a regular practice for most families. Church-going was woven into the fabric of community life, whether it was a weekly habit or just part of a holiday tradition. But times change and for many people, the concept of church belongs to a bygone era when families sat down to dinner every night and baseball was still the nation's favorite pastime.

You may have childhood memories of church—or you may never have set foot inside a church until (or after!) you became a Christian. Whatever your past experience has been, you will find new meaning to church as you grow and discover your place in the family of God. Some people think they can get plenty of spiritual input from Christian videos, radio, music, books, and podcasts. Although these can be beneficial, they are no substitute for fellowship and personal involvement with other believers.

The Bible says that the church is like being part of a body (see 1 Corinthians 12:12). We are one body, with many different parts—and every part is important. That means God has a special purpose for you in your local church. With God's help, you can discover and fulfill that purpose.

You can begin to do this now by letting God's Word shape your understanding of why church is important and how you will respond.

Read 1 Corinthians 12:27 and write it down here:

_____

_____

Read Ephesians 4:16 and write it down here:

_____

_____

Looking back over this session, what is the most important discovery you have made about the importance of church?

_____

_____

RESPOND

If you are committed to growing in your Christian faith, take some practical steps:

- Find a church home and make it a priority to attend every week. Sunday Worship service begins at:

  _____

- Is there a Bible study or class to attend? Note the day and time:

  _____

- Look for opportunities for fellowship. Read the church bulletin or contact the church office for more information.

- You have God-given gifts and abilities. Look around your church for opportunities to serve. Think of some practical ways you can help in your church. List them here:

_____

_____

_____

_____

SCRIPTURE MEMORY
We are carefully joined together in him, becoming a holy temple for the Lord.
—Ephesians 2:21

CHAPTER 3

I've Never Done That out Loud!
WORSHIP AND PRAYER

Your new faith in Christ is bringing about changes in your life—have you noticed? Of course you have! You have peace inside, knowing that God loves you and has accepted you as His child—because Jesus Christ died for you. That empty place in your spirit has been filled by the only One who can satisfy the deepest need of every heart. God has come to live in and with you, and this new relationship will affect every part of your life.

There's a Christian term for the changes you're experiencing. It's called *spiritual transformation*. In fairy tales, transformation takes place instantly. You know, the frog becomes a prince with one kiss. Snow White awakens from her deep sleep. Pinocchio becomes a real boy. But life is not a fairy tale and most changes don't come overnight. Now don't misunderstand—when you asked Jesus to forgive your sin and to come live in your heart, your salvation was instantaneous. You were completely forgiven and given a new life. The apostle Paul told the believers in Corinth, "Anyone who belongs to Christ has become a new person. The old life is gone; a new life has begun!" (2 Corinthians 5:17).

This new life is what you are now growing in. As you learn more about God and His love for you, it transforms your thinking and stirs up a desire to do things you may have had no interest in before, like reading the Bible, praying, or going to church. Before you became a Christian, attending a church service may have felt uncomfortable; especially if people lifted their hands while singing or held hands in prayer. Part of the *spiritual transformation* you experience as a Christian comes when you recognize that God attaches great importance to worship and prayer. Why? Because these are the deepest, most honest expressions of love and faith we can offer to God.

The Bible teaches us that the God who does not need anything nevertheless desires the adoration and worship of His created children.
—A. W. Tozer

In this session, you will begin to discover:
- The worship God desires
- The purpose of prayer

Before you start, be sure to pray. A simple prayer might go something like this:

Lord, I'm so thankful to be Your child.
The more I know about You, the more I see how wonderful You are.
Please draw me close to You in worship and teach me how to pray.

READ

We were made to worship. Deep within the DNA of the human spirit is a desire to worship. The Bible tells us that God has "planted eternity in the human heart" (Ecclesiastes 3:11). What does that mean? In simple terms, it means God created people with a sense of something greater than themselves—something more to life than this life.

God gave human beings the innate capacity to know, love, and worship Him. This has been described as a "God-shaped hole" in humanity's heart; a spiritual vacuum that no one or nothing else can fill. When people try to fill this place with anything else, they are worshipping a god of their own choosing. It may be another person, possessions, or pursuits. Some people fill this place with themselves and their own desires.

What is worship? The word comes from the old English word *worth-ship*, which means to attribute great honor and esteem to someone who merits it. Worship expresses itself in complete devotion to the object of its love. God is perfect in everything He is and does. He alone deserves our worship. Jesus said, "You shall worship the LORD your God, and Him only you shall serve" (Matthew 4:10 NKJV).

But what does it mean to worship? Is it something we do only on Sundays in church? Is it only expressed through songs and prayers? In our desire to worship God and give Him the honor He alone deserves, how can we begin to know what pleases Him?

- **Discover the Worship God Desires**

    Hebrews 13:15–16 is a good place to start. This Scripture teaches us three important principles about worship that pleases God.

Therefore, let us offer through Jesus a continual sacrifice of praise to God, proclaiming our allegiance to his name. And don't forget to do good and to share with those in need. These are the sacrifices that please God. (NLT)

1. **Proclaim.** God is pleased when we worship Him with our voices. How can we use our voice to worship God? Read the following verses for the answers.

    Psalm 105:1–2 _____

    Ephesians 5:19 _____

    Colossians 3:16 _____

2. **Do good.** God is pleased when we worship Him through our actions. The way we live our lives must show we truly worship God—not just on Sunday, but every day. What do the following verses teach you about worship in action?

    Matthew 5:16 _____

    Ephesians 5:1–2 _____

3. **Share.** God is pleased when we worship Him through giving and serving. The word *share* as it is used here has several layers of meaning. It includes giving of yourself: your time, talent, energy, and financial resources. Read the following verses and note what they say about this expression of worship.

    1 Corinthians 12:4–7 _____

    Proverbs 3:9–10 _____

    2 Corinthians 9:10–13 _____

Worship is practical. It happens before church, and it happens after church. Worship is not only singing; it's serving.
—Greg Laurie

- **Discover the Purpose of Prayer**

    Prayer has become a subject of growing interest in recent years. Studies have been performed in an effort to discover if prayer can actually affect the outcome of physical ailments. Medical researchers acknowledge that prayer contributes to physical and emotional well-being. But there is a great deal of confusion as to what prayer actually is.

    Prayer is not tapping into some unknown mystical force, or energy that we stir up in ourselves. Prayer is simply talking to God. As a growing believer, you have the privilege of coming to God with all your concerns and requests. You can—and should—speak to God about anything and everything. He will listen and answer. Prayer is an essential ingredient in growing your new relationship with Jesus Christ, so take a few minutes to discover some basic things about prayer.

    When? The Bible tells us to pray "morning, noon, and night" (Psalm 55:17). There is no time of the day or night when you cannot talk to God.

    Why? Why do we pray in Jesus' name? (see 1 Timothy 2:5):

    _____

    _____

    What? What should we include in our prayers? Read the verses below for some answers:

    Psalm 100:3–4 _____

    Psalm 51:2; 1 John 1:9 _____

    Psalm 120:1 _____

    Philippians 4:6 _____

    1 Timothy 2:1 _____

    James 1:5 _____

How? How can we be certain that God will hear and answer our prayers?

John 15:7 _____

1 John 3:22 _____

1 John 5:14–15 _____

Prayer is not just trying to get God to move. It is an important process through which God moves and changes us. In other words, prayer will not only transform whatever you are praying about; it will transform you.
—Greg Laurie

REFLECT

Have you ever been drawn into the kitchen by some delicious aroma? Think of cinnamon rolls baking in the oven, sizzling bacon, or the welcoming scent of freshly-brewed coffee. Just breathing it in compels you to the source.

Did you know that worship and prayer is a fragrance that God finds irresistible? If you wonder what this means, look at the picture of worship in the Old Testament. The detailed plans God gave Moses for building the tent of meeting included an altar in front of the "Most Holy Place" (see Exodus 26:33-34). Every morning and every night, Aaron the priest would burn aromatic incense on the altar, so there would be "perpetual incense before the LORD" (Exodus 30:8 NKJV). God Himself gave the formula for this sweet smelling savor.

In Scripture, incense is a symbol for prayer. The book of Revelation gives us a glimpse of the prayers of God's people, mixed with incense, rising before God's throne (see Revelation 8:3–4). As you reflect on what it means to worship and pray, remember that your Creator enjoys the sweet scent of praise.

Write down Psalm 141:2 and make it your own prayer. _____
_____
_____

Looking back over this session, what is the most important discovery you have made about the importance of worship and prayer?

_____

_____

_____

RESPOND

Will you worship? Think about your everyday dealings and responsibilities. How can these activities become acts of worship? Write down one thing you will do this week to:

Proclaim: _____

Do good: _____

Share: _____

Will you pray? Christians need to practice prayer. That doesn't mean you rehearse spiritual phrases until your prayers sound impressive. It means that you exercise your privilege *daily* to talk *with* God. Make a plan to practice this week.

I will start each day thanking God for: _____

I will ask the Lord's help with: _____

I will ask a friend to pray with me about: _____

SCRIPTURE MEMORY

Enter his gates with thanksgiving; go into his courts with praise.
—Psalm 100:4

CHAPTER 4

I Have Good News!
SHARING YOUR FAITH

In life, we come in contact with many people on many different levels. Those who know us best are our family and close friends. They've seen us in the good times and bad, through years and countless experiences. Neighbors know us, even if only by face or name. Others know us in a specific role, such as coworker, employer, fellow student, or club member. Then there are the people we have only passing contact with, like the passenger in the seat next to you on an airplane or that couple you always see on your morning walk. These are the people Jesus had in mind when He said, "Go into all the world and preach the Good News to everyone" (Mark 16:15). So how does that happen?

For most of us, the thought of witnessing induces a heart-thumping, knee-knocking reaction. We just don't know where to begin or what to say. We're reluctant for fear of being rejected or put on the spot if we can't answer their questions. As a new believer, you may feel like you should wait until you know the Bible better, but all you need to begin sharing your faith with others is a changed heart. The Bible tells the story of a blind man whom Jesus healed (see John 9:1–41). When the religious leaders heard about it, they began to ask the man challenging questions—to which he replied, "I know this: I was blind, and now I can see!"

As you study the Bible and continue to grow in your walk with Jesus, you will be able to answer more questions than you can now. The place to begin is by simply sharing what you know.

In this session, you will begin to discover:

- Power to share your faith
- How to share a simple message
- How to share a personal message

Before you start, be sure to pray. A simple prayer might go something like this:

Lord, thank You for saving me. I'm grateful that someone took time to share the gospel with me. Please help me to share the Good News with others, as You have said to do.

READ

Some people approach witnessing as though they were selling a product. Their efforts come across like a sales pitch. If the person doesn't respond, they feel like a failure. In reality, we are more like the postal service. We're responsible to deliver the message, but it's up to the recipient to respond. We may be able to *lead* people to Christ—but *He* is the only one who can save them. Jesus said, "No one can come to Me unless the Father who sent Me draws him" (John 6:44 NASB).

- **Discover Power to Share Your Faith**

    There is nothing we can do to convert a person, but the Lord will give us power to be witnesses for Jesus Christ. Where does this power come from, and what will be the result?

    Acts 1:8 _____

    Acts 4:31 _____

    You may still feel nervous when you share your faith, but you can be sure the Holy Spirit will help you. God never asks us to do anything without giving us strength to do it.

    Like the apostle Paul, you can say, "For I can do everything through Christ, who gives me strength" (Philippians 4:13).

- **Discover How to Share a Simple Message**

The Holy Spirit gives us power to witness, and there is power in the Word of God. The apostle Paul wrote, "I am not ashamed of the gospel of Christ, for it is the power of God to salvation for everyone who believes" (Romans 1:16 NKJV). He also told the church in Rome that "faith comes from hearing, that is, hearing the Good News about Christ" (Romans 10:17).

God promises that His Word will not return to Him without accomplishing His purpose (see Isaiah 55:10–11). This is why we must read God's Word and begin to memorize it, so that our sharing will be effective. This doesn't mean we wait to share until we have large blocks of Scripture memorized. It does mean that we'll be continually learning, adding to our storehouse of Scripture.

Here are four Scriptures to help you share the gospel in a simple message. We must:

Realize we're all sinners. Romans 3:23 says: _____

Recognize Jesus as Savior. Romans 5:8 says: _____

*Repen*t of our sin. Acts 3:19 says: _____

Receive Jesus as Savior. Romans 10:13 says: _____

- **Discover How to Share a Personal Message**

There is more to sharing our faith than words. In fact, we may be skilled in telling people how to receive Christ and still be a very poor witness. Sharing our faith must be a way of life. Remember those people we come in contact with in everyday life? They may hear our words, but more often than not it's our *life* they're listening to.

How can our personal life be a powerful witness? Read the following verses for the answer.

Matthew 5:13–16 _____

Colossians 4:5–6 _____

1 Peter 3:15 _____

REFLECT

Let's go back to our opening thought. Jesus said, "Preach the Good News to everyone." If we sincerely want to obey the Lord on this point, we need to see the big picture. The fact is, being a witness is something you *do*, and it's also something you *are*.

To put it another way, you can share your faith 24 hours a day, seven days a week, 365 days a year. At times, you consciously share your faith—more often, you silently witness by the way you live. It has been said, "Preach the gospel—and if necessary, use words." Jesus said we must be "salt and light" to those around us (see Matthew 5:13–16).

Salt affects whatever it touches. Salt also stimulates thirst. By living a godly life, we can have a positive influence and stimulate spiritual thirst in someone else. When light shines, it draws the eye away from darkness. By sharing God's Word, we're holding a light up for all to see.

You will have opportunities to speak about your faith or share your personal testimony. Work at being prepared to share the gospel message "in season and out of season" as 2 Timothy 4:2 tells us (NIV). Don't be afraid to ask the Lord to open doors for you to share your faith. The Holy Spirit will lead you to the right person at the right time—and He will help you know what to say.

Looking back over this session, what is the most important discovery you have made about sharing your faith?

_____

_____

_____

RESPOND

Do you want to share your faith? Why not ask the Lord for power to be His witness right now? Begin to pray, by name, for three people who need to know Christ.

1. _____
2. _____
3. _____

Consider ways you can share your faith (by word and by deed) with them. Write some practical ideas down.

_____

_____

_____

Prepare your own "One-Minute Message." Use the guidelines provided on the next page for help with this.

HOW TO SHARE YOUR
One-Minute Message

Your personal testimony is a resource to help you build bridges, instead of burning them, when sharing the gospel with others. It lets people see that you were once in their shoes, but have now been transformed by the power of Christ.
—Greg Laurie

Three Keys to the One-Minute Message

1. My Life Before Christ

Don't glorify your past, but mention how you were before Christ. Use simple words to describe how you felt (e.g., empty, hopeless, guilty, lost, self-centered).

_____

_____

_____

2. My Life Changed by Christ

Summarize how you came into a relationship with Christ. Be sure to mention the key elements of the gospel.

- "I *realized* that I was a sinner" (see Romans 3:23)
- "I *recognized* that Jesus died for my sins" (see Romans 5:8)
- "I *repented* or turned away from my sins" (see Acts 3:19)
- "I *received* Jesus Christ as my Savior" (see Romans 10:13)

_____

_____

_____

3. **My New Life in Christ.**

   Tell how your life has changed now that you have a personal relationship with Christ. Use phrases any person can understand (e.g., "I now have peace," "I have found a purpose in life," "I no longer feel empty," or "I have learned where to go for help with life's problems").

   _____

   _____

   _____

SCRIPTURE MEMORY

Give thanks to the LORD and proclaim his greatness.
Let the whole world know what he has done.

—Psalm 105:1

CHAPTER 5

Decisions, Decisions
KNOWING AND DOING GOD'S WILL

When we bring up the topic of God's will, we may have two views that are not accurate. View number one is that finding God's will is really hard. God's sort of hiding it from us. And we think the Lord is up there saying, "You're getting warmer. Warmer. Hot. Hot. No. Cold. Cold. Cold."

Or the opposite view is: We think God's will is something undesirable. It's not good, sort of like a diet. We may think, "Oh, if it's God's will it can't be good. It can't be desirable. It's going to be bad. It's going to be miserable."

But the truth is that God wants to reveal His will, and we're most joyful when we're in His will.

In this session, you will begin to discover:

- Some important basics of God's will
- God's will for every believer
- How to know God's will

Before you start, be sure to pray. A simple prayer might go something like this:

Lord, I know You love me and that Your will is perfect.
I want to learn and obey Your will.
Please reveal Your will for my life.

READ

The Bible often describes people as being like sheep. While this is not the most flattering description, it's accurate! For one thing, sheep are simple creatures with a herd mentality. They are easily driven along, following wherever the moving masses go. How many choices do we make in life simply because "everybody" is doing it?

As followers of Jesus, we are sheep following our Good Shepherd. Jesus said, "My sheep listen to my voice; I know them, and they follow me" (John 10:27).

Jesus' flock ought to know when He speaks to them. But what are the characteristics of God's "voice"?

- **Discover Some Important Basics of God's Will**

    God's will is always in harmony with God's Word. Knowing God's will begins with knowing what the Bible says. If our desire conflicts with the plain teaching of the Bible, it cannot be the will of God. Obviously, the Bible doesn't spell out what to do in every specific situation. But as we learn more from God's Word, we will grow to think and see things according to God's perspective.

    Why can you depend on God's Word to know God's will?

    Psalm 119:105 _____

    2 Timothy 3:16 _____

    To know God's will, you need to be filled with the Holy Spirit. The apostle Paul said this to the Christians in Ephesus, "So then do not be foolish, but understand what the will of the Lord is. And do not get drunk with wine, for that is dissipation, but be filled with the Spirit" (Ephesians 5:17–18 NASB). Paul makes a clear comparison here. A person controlled by alcohol behaves foolishly. But a person controlled by the Holy Spirit behaves wisely, understanding the Lord's will.

    In His earthly ministry, Jesus was filled with the Spirit and was led by the Spirit (see Luke 4:1). All through the Book of Acts, you will find examples of God's Spirit personally leading God's servants. We can be certain God is leading us in His will when His Spirit is in control of our lives.

You will learn more about the Holy Spirit in another session. For now, what did Jesus promise the Holy Spirit will do for every believer?

John 16:13–15 _____

- ## Discover God's Will for Every Believer

What is God's will for every believer? Simply put, Christians should be different! Our lives should be marked by increasing obedience to God's Word. The verses below address some areas of life where God's will is clear and certain for every believer. Make it personal—what is God's will for *you*?

Titus 2:11–13 _____

1 Thessalonians 4:3 _____

Colossians 3:8–9 _____

Colossians 3:12–14 _____

1 Thessalonians 5:16–18 _____

- ## Discover How to Know God's Will

You might be asking yourself, *How can I really be sure that I know God's will?* You can be sure that God will show you His plan *because He said He would.* God repeats this promise again and again in His Word. Listen to what He says in Isaiah 48:17: "I am the LORD your God, who teaches you what is good for you and leads you along the paths you should follow."

He will not let you stumble around in the dark (see Isaiah 42:16) and if you get off track, He will call you back (see Isaiah 30:21), saying, "This is the way you should go,' whether to the right or to the left."

That doesn't mean God audibly speaks to you every morning, saying, "Okay, here's the plan for today." He just leads us a step at a time. That's because God's will is not an itinerary; it's an attitude. We shouldn't overly mystify it.

The surest way to know God's will for the future is by being obedient in what you know today. God's way becomes clear when we start walking in it. Romans 12:2 tells us, "And do not be conformed to this world, but be transformed by the renewing of your mind, that you may prove what is that good and acceptable and perfect will of God" (NKJV).

God will speak through His Word. As we have already said, God will never guide you in a way that is contrary to His Word. So every idea, every decision, every teaching can be tested by the Word of God in order to know whether it is wrong or right. This doesn't mean you just randomly open your Bible, looking for an answer that "fits" your question. That's a dangerous and faulty method for determining God's will. Better to take the time to read and understand God's Word, and then He will speak to you.

According to Psalm 119:165, what will the person who depends on God's Word for guidance experience?

_____

_____

God will speak through circumstances. Ephesians 1:11 tells us that God "works all things after the counsel of His will" (NASB). God can obviously use circumstances if He chooses to, and the Bible shows that He does. For example, Joseph's jealous brothers sold him into slavery. We would be quick to say he was a victim of circumstances—but Joseph came to see that it was all part of God's plan (see Genesis 45:5).

God will open up opportunities to live out His will in our lives. Sometimes God has a divine appointment for us to share the gospel with someone. Sometimes a tough circumstance is an opportunity to grow in obedience, though it may be hard. We must be careful to follow the promptings of his Holy Spirit. We are called to walk by faith, not by sight (see 2 Corinthians 5:7).

According to Romans 8:28, how should we view circumstances?

_____

_____

_____

God will speak to your heart. When you feel your heart stirring, compelling you toward action, what should you do? First, remember that every impression that comes from God will line up with His Word. Second, if you are being led by God, you will have the peace of God.

Colossians 3:15 says, "Let the peace of Christ rule in your hearts" (NASB).

The word *rule* gives the sense of letting God's peace act as an umpire, conclusively settling a matter.

Finally, remember that, while seeking God's will is not always easy, His will is always good. We may not always like it. We may not always agree with it. But God promises to supply all our needs in Christ (see Ephesians 3:20).

Never be afraid to commit an unknown future to a known God.
—Greg Laurie

REFLECT

Christian writer Elisabeth Elliot tells about a young woman who went to her pastor for counsel. Struggling to know what God wanted her to do with her life, she confided that her effort to balance her desire to do God's will and pursue her goals was leaving her frustrated. The pastor took out a slip of paper, wrote two words and handed it to her with simple instructions. "Choose one of these words to cross out." She glanced down and read *No Lord*. Which to cross out? It didn't take long for her to see that if she was saying *No*, she could not say *Lord*; and if she wanted to say *Lord*, she could not say *No*.

Life is filled with people like this young woman, looking for direction. We all want our story to have a happy ending, but it's hard to turn over the rights to all our plans and decisions. Yet this is what we must do to find God's will. As the old hymn says, we need to "trust and obey, for there's no other way to be happy in Jesus."

"'For I know the plans I have for you,' declares the LORD, 'plans to prosper you and not to harm you, plans to give you hope and a future'" (Jeremiah 29:11 NIV). This is God's promise to you! Don't be afraid to completely surrender your will to Him. You can trust Him with your life.

Write down Proverbs 3:5–6 and make it your prayer.

_____

_____

_____

Looking back over this session, what is the most important discovery you have made about knowing and doing God's will?

_____

_____

_____

RESPOND

You wrote Proverbs 3:5–6 down as a prayer. Here are some practical ways to live it.

- When you pray, always ask God for His will to overrule your own.
- Seek God, in prayer and in His Word, *before* you make a decision.
- Obey God without hesitation.

What is the most important decision or choice you are facing in your life right now?

_____

_____

What steps will you take to discover God's will in this matter?

_____

_____

SCRIPTURE MEMORY

I will instruct you and teach you in the way you should go;
I will counsel you with my loving eye on you.
—Psalm 32:8 NIV

DECISIONS, DECISIONS . . . WHAT THE BIBLE SAYS ABOUT

Anger
Proverbs 15:1; Proverbs 29:11; Colossians 3:8; James 1:19–20

Anxiety
Matthew 6:33–34; Philippians 4:6–7; 1 Peter 5:7

Bad Habits
Psalm 119:11; Romans 6:11–14; James 4:7–8

Childrearing
Deuteronomy 6:6–7; Proverbs 22:6; Ephesians 6:1–4; Colossians 3:21

Depression
Isaiah 53:4–5; Lamentations 3:19–24; 2 Corinthians 4:8–9

Divorce
Malachi 2:14–16; Matthew 19:3–9; 1 Corinthians 7

Envy
Genesis 4:3–6; Proverbs 14:30; 1 Corinthians 3:3; Hebrews 13:5

False Teaching
Colossians 2:8–9; 1 Timothy 4:16; 2 Timothy 2:15; 1 John 4:1–3

Friendships
1 Corinthians 15:33; 2 Corinthians 6:14; Philippians 2:3–4

Finances
Malachi 3:8-10; Matthew 6:33; 2 Corinthians 9:7; Philippians 4:19

Forgiveness
Psalm 32; Psalm 51; Isaiah 43:25; Colossians 3:13; 1 John 1:9

Guilt
Proverbs 28:13; Isaiah 44:22; John 8:36; Romans 8:1

Knowing God's Will
Psalm 37:3, 5; John 14:15; John 16:13; Philippians 4:6–7

Marriage
Genesis 2:18; Proverbs 18:22; 2 Corinthians 6:14; Ephesians 5:22–33

Obedience
Deuteronomy 11:26–28; Luke 6:46–49; John 14:15, 21; 1 John 2:5

Patience
Psalm 37:7; 1 Corinthians 13:4; Galatians 5:22; Philippians 4:11; James 1:2–4

Prayer
Matthew 6:6; John 15:7; John 16:24; Philippians 4:6, 19; Colossians 4:2

Sexual Purity
1 Corinthians 6:15–20; Ephesians 5:3; Colossians 3:5; Romans 6:12–14

Temptation
1 Corinthians 10:13; Romans 12:1-2; James 1:13; James 4:7

Tithing
Proverbs 3:9–10; Malachi 3:10; Matthew 6:2-4; Luke 6:38; Philippians 4:19

Worldliness
Matthew 6:33; Romans 12:1–2; Colossians 3:1–2; 1 John 2:15–17

CHAPTER 6

Growing Pains
TRIALS AND TEMPTATIONS

Because you are growing in your new faith, your old way of living no longer fits. You need to replace natural impulses and old patterns of behavior with new attitudes and desires. The Bible describes this as a new nature that God has created in you. The apostle Paul says in his letter to the Colossians,

You have stripped off your old sinful nature and all its wicked deeds. Put on your new nature, and be renewed as you learn to know your Creator and become like him. (Colossians 3:9–10 NLT)

Once you became a Christian, God gave you His Holy Spirit to help you live and grow in your new spiritual nature. As you begin to live what you learn, change will come. Now understand, this isn't a spiritual "self-improvement" program. When we try to live a godly life in our own strength, we fail miserably. God wants us to rely on the power of the Holy Spirit to overcome our old, sinful nature.

That brings us to the topic of this session. Some Christians mistakenly think that following Jesus means they are leaving all their problems behind—that life will be filled with blue skies and green lights. This is not the case. As a follower of Jesus, you will still encounter trials and temptations. The good news is that for the child of God, even painful or unpleasant experiences serve a purpose in helping our faith to grow.

In this session, you will begin to discover:

- The difference between temptation and trials
- How to resist temptation
- How to persevere in trials

Before you start, be sure to pray. A simple prayer might go something like this:

Lord, please help me learn to walk in the new nature You are creating in me. By the power of the Holy Spirit, please help me to resist temptation, and grow through every trial that comes my way.

READ

Remember, God has given you His Holy Spirit so you can grow in your new spiritual nature. You need to know that your old, sinful nature will still fight for control. When you trusted Christ to save you from sin, you defected from Satan's army. The devil doesn't want you to actually realize that sin's power over you has been broken. He will assault you with doubts and try to hinder your spiritual growth. *But he is a defeated enemy.* As Ephesians 6:10 says, "Be strong in the Lord and in the power of His might" (NKJV).

- **Discover the difference between temptation and trials.**

    There is a difference between being tempted and being tested (trials). Simply put, the purpose of a temptation is to entice you and draw you into sin. The purpose of a trial, or test, is to develop godly character or strengthen your faith.

    Every trial you face is an opportunity to trust God. Sometimes, however, you may feel angry or think God has deserted you. You are being tempted to turn your back on God and miss out on what He wants to develop in you. The devil wants to hold you back from growing. As Jesus said in John 10:10, the devil is a "thief" who wants to "steal and kill and destroy."

    Read James 1:13 and explain why God will never tempt you.

    ___

    Read James 1:2–4 and explain why God will allow you to experience trials (tests).

    ___

- **Discover how to resist temptation.**

    Where does temptation come from? The Bible teaches that Satan is the tempter with demonic forces who do his bidding (see Ephesians 6:11–12). The devil's strategy includes using the "world" and the "flesh." *What does this mean?*

The "world" refers to a way of thinking that is hostile to God. In 2 Corinthians 4:4, the devil is called "the god of this world" who "has blinded the minds of those who don't believe."

What temptations does the world offer? Read 1 John 2:16 for the answer.

The "flesh" refers to our old nature, which is influenced by the world. In James 1:14–15, we learn that, "Temptation comes from our own desires, which entice us and drag us away. These desires give birth to sinful actions. And when sin is allowed to grow, it gives birth to death." When we give in to any temptation, we can't blame the devil. He may get us to "think about it," but we are the ones who listen, desire, and give in to what he offers. *Never put the welcome mat out to an evil thought*.

It isn't a sin to be tempted, for even Jesus faced temptation. But when you begin to *entertain* the thought in your mind, you open the door to sin. How can temptation be resisted and overcome? Read the following verses for the answer.

1 Corinthians 10:13 _____

James 4:7–10 _____

- ### Discover how to persevere in trials.

Usually, our first response to difficulty is to ask, "Why me?" We don't understand what God is doing. Life's lessons often come with thorny circumstances. Some crisis, loss, or drastic change occurs. You may not feel God's presence. Your prayers seem to go unanswered. You may wonder if God is punishing you or has simply forgotten about you.

Unlike temptation, where running away is definitely the best option, God means for us to persevere—*hang in there*—through times of testing. We may not get an answer for all of our "whys," but we can take comfort in knowing that God only allows difficulties in our life to cause our faith to grow. He wants us to learn to live by faith, not by feelings.

Read the following passages to learn the purpose for trials.

1 Peter 1:7 _____

James 1:2–4 _____

2 Corinthians 1:3–7 _____

What can you be certain of when going through a trial?

John 16:33 _____

Luke 6:47–48 _____

2 Corinthians 4:7–18 _____

What does God promise when you are going through a trial?

Psalm 55:22 _____

Isaiah 41:10 _____

Trust in God. Becoming a believer will not take away all the problems in your life—but it gives you new perspective, new trust, and new hope in what God is going to do in and through you as a result of every difficulty you encounter.
—**Greg Laurie**

REFLECT

One of nature's most fascinating miracles is the transformation of an ordinary caterpillar into a graceful butterfly. You wouldn't guess that such an earthbound insect could ever take flight on delicate wings. The change begins when the caterpillar goes into a chrysalis, or cocoon, where metamorphosis takes place. When it's time to emerge, the young butterfly works hard to break through the chrysalis. This struggle is necessary because, without it, the butterfly will not have fully developed its strength. Any attempt to "help" the butterfly escape will leave it weak and unable to fly. It's a painful process that is ultimately good for one of God's most delicate wonders.

Why does God allow trials and temptations to be part of our Christian life? God allows them because He can work ultimate good into our lives. There will be things you go through that you will not understand. When you struggle for answers to your "whys"—or for power to say no to temptation—remember that God is forming you into the image of His Son, Jesus Christ. God permits the struggle so you will emerge from the chrysalis of testing with fully developed faith and the strength to live a godly life.

Write down James 1:3–4 and make it your prayer.

_____

_____

_____

Looking back over this session, what is the most important discovery you have made about trials and temptation?

_____

_____

_____

RESPOND

How will you deal with the growing pains of your new life in Christ? With the help of the Holy Spirit, old problems have new solutions. Your old nature still fights for control and doesn't need much encouragement. But every time you obey God and resist sin, your new nature grows stronger.

The devil will hit you with temptation when you are most vulnerable (e.g., tired, lonely, frustrated, afraid, overconfident, bored). Here are four practical ways to avoid and resist temptation:

1. Humble yourself before God (see James 4:7). Acknowledge His authority in your life and confess your weaknesses to Him. Sincerely ask God to help you stay away from people, places, and situations that may tempt you.

2. Resist the devil (see James 4:7). When Satan tempted Jesus in the wilderness, Jesus responded back with Scripture (see Matthew 4:1–11). Knowing God's Word in your heart and in your head will protect you against the devil's assault. Begin to memorize Scripture to combat temptation and endure trials.

3. Draw close to God (see James 4:8). The more time you spend with the Lord through Bible study, worship, and prayer, the less likely you will be to give in when temptation comes.

4. Wash your hands and purify your heart (see James 4:8). When the Holy Spirit convicts you of any sin, don't rationalize it—repent! Harboring unconfessed sin gives the devil a foothold in your life.

What practical steps will you take to avoid and resist temptation? List *specific* changes that need to be made in the area of:

Your thought life _____

Your habits _____

Your relationships _____

SCRIPTURE MEMORY

No temptation has overtaken you except what is common to mankind. And God is faithful; he will not let you be tempted beyond what you can bear. But when you are tempted, he will also provide a way out so that you can endure it.
—1 Corinthians 10:13 NIV

CHAPTER 7

Trinity 101
A BEGINNER'S GUIDE TO GOD'S NATURE

Who is God? That's not an easy question to answer, because it requires that we try to wrap our finite minds around an infinite God. So the best place to begin is to accept that we cannot fully understand who God is or why He does certain things. The Bible promises that the time will come when everything about God is made perfectly clear (see 1 Corinthians 13:12). Until then, we can trust that God, who is too big for our minds to contain, is near and wants to be known. In Jeremiah 24:7, the Lord said, "I will give them a heart to know Me, that I am the LORD" (NKJV).

While it's impossible to understand everything, we can and should devote a lifetime to discovering more about our incomprehensible God. Everything we need to know can be found in the pages of His Word.

In this session, you will begin to discover:

- The attributes of God
- God's nature as Father, Son, and Holy Spirit

Before you start, be sure to pray. A simple prayer might go something like this:

Lord, I want to know more about You.
You are greater than my mind can ever comprehend,
but I believe the Bible reveals who You are and how You can be known.
Please help me to know and love You better every day.

READ

What does God look like? A teacher told the class to draw a picture of what made them happy. One little boy kept drawing, long after everybody else had handed in their picture. The teacher asked what he was drawing. Without looking up, he said, "God." She gently told him that no one knows what God looks like. Unhesitating, he answered, "They will when I'm through!"

While you will never see a photograph of God, you can find sketches of Him throughout Scripture. God has drawn a picture of Himself in His Word that allows us to see the character and nature of who He is.

- **Discover the attributes of God.**

    The Bible reveals some characteristics that can be attributed only to God. While it's impossible to understand God completely, knowing these truths deepens our faith and increases our trust in God. Take time to consider some of these characteristics.

    Read the following Scriptures and fill in the blanks.

    God is eternal. While believers will live forever (immortality), only God is eternal. God was not created. God exists outside of time and there has never been a time when God did not exist.

    Take a moment to look up and complete the following Scripture reference.

    Psalm 90:2: "Before the mountains were born, before you gave birth to the earth and the world _____ you are God."

    Also read: 2 Peter 3:8 and Revelation 1:8.

    God is all-knowing. The Bible teaches that God is omniscient, which means He has complete and perfect knowledge. He doesn't need to learn anything new or have anything explained. He knows everything that has happened, everything taking place now, and everything that will happen in the future.

    Look up the following Bible verse and fill in the missing parts.

Hebrews 4:13: "Nothing in all creation is hidden from God. Everything is _____ and ____ _____ before his eyes."

Also read: Psalm 139:1–6; Matthew 6:8; John 16:30.

God is ever-present. The Bible teaches that God is omnipresent, which means He is present everywhere at all times. There is no place in the universe that God does not see. His presence is everywhere.

Look up the following Bible verse and fill in the missing parts.

Jeremiah 23:24: "'Can anyone hide from me in a secret place? Am I not _____ in all the _____ and _____?' says the LORD."

Also read: Psalm 139:7–12 and Proverbs 15:3.

God is all-powerful. The Bible teaches that God is omnipotent, which means that He can do anything that does not contradict His nature. There is no challenge too difficult for Him, no circumstance out of His control, and no problem beyond His ability to solve. There is no one more powerful than God.

Jeremiah 32:27: "I am the LORD, the God of all the peoples of the world. Is anything _____ for me?"

Also read: Job 42:2; Psalm 62:11; Matthew 19:26.

God is unchanging. The Bible teaches that God is immutable, which means He does not change in character or in His promises. Because He is perfect in all His ways and faithful to His Word, God's dealings with humankind are righteous and just. We can count on God's unchanging love.

Take a moment to look up and complete the following Scripture reference.

Malachi 3:6: "I am the LORD, and I _____ _____ ."

Also read: Hebrews 1:10–12; Hebrews 13:8; James 1:17.

- **Discover God's Nature as Father, Son, and Holy Spirit**

    The Bible teaches that there is only one true God. He is the Creator and Sustainer of the universe, the only God that exists. In Isaiah 43:10–11, God says to "believe in me, and understand that I alone am God. There is no other God—there never has been, and there never will be. I, yes I, am the LORD, and there is no other Savior."

    At the same time, within the nature of the one true God, there are three distinct and eternal persons: the Father, the Son, and the Holy Spirit.

    ## GOD THE FATHER

    God is called the Father in both the Old and New Testaments. The Lord Himself spoke of His relationship with His people, saying, "I am a Father to Israel . . ." (Jeremiah 31:9 NKJV). Jesus called God "My Father" (see John 20:17) and taught His disciples to pray to "Our Father in heaven" (see Matthew 6:9).

    Being able to relate to God as Father helps us to understand His caring relationship and loving authority over His people. What do the following verses tell you about the nature of our heavenly Father?

    Psalm 68:5 _____

    John 17:11 _____

    Matthew 6:31–33 _____

    Luke 15:11–32 _____

    ## GOD THE SON

    The Bible undeniably teaches that the Son, Jesus Christ, is God. Jesus did not become God—He has always been God. Speaking of His participation in the creation of all things, the apostle John declares that Jesus existed before time began (see John 1:1–4). Jesus Himself said, "'Before Abraham was, I AM'" (John 8:58 NKJV).

    Jesus came to earth with a specific mission: to pay the penalty for our sins by dying in our place. To do this, He became fully human while still remaining divine. Simply put, Jesus is God in human form. What do the following verses tell you about the nature of the Son, Jesus Christ?

John 1:14 _____

Philippians 2:5–11 _____

Colossians 1:15–17 _____

Hebrews 4:14–16; 5:8–9 _____

GOD THE HOLY SPIRIT

When Jesus returned to the Father, He promised He would send "another Helper, that He may be with you forever" (John 14:16 NASB). In Greek, the word *another* means "another of the same kind." Jesus promised to send a Helper who was just like Him. This Helper is God the Holy Spirit. The Bible teaches that the Holy Spirit is not an impersonal power, but a Person. The Holy Spirit is the third Person of the Trinity.

When you accepted Jesus Christ as your Lord and Savior, the Holy Spirit came to live within you (see 1 Corinthians 6:19). His presence is God's "seal" that you belong to Him (see Ephesians 1:13–14). His presence and power in your life enables you to grow in your new relationship with God. What do the following verses tell you about the nature of the Holy Spirit?

John 14:16–17 _____

John 14:26 _____

1 Corinthians 2:10–12 _____

Romans 8:26–27 _____

REFLECT

Have you ever gazed up into a wilderness night sky? Something in the silent majesty of countless stars quiets the human heart in awe. David expressed this wonder and worship in Psalm 8:3–4, saying, "When I look at the night sky and see the work of your fingers—the moon and the stars you set in place—what are mere mortals that you should think about them, human beings that you should care for them?"

We worship a God who is greater than our minds can grasp or our language describe. But faith can embrace what our intellect can't comprehend. Our Creator—the all-knowing, all-powerful, ever-present, eternal, and unchanging God—has given you a heart to know Him. He promises that, "If you look for me wholeheartedly, you will find me" (Jeremiah 29:13).

As you reflect on who God is, remember that He is always thinking about you. What does Psalm 139:17–18 tell you about God's thoughts toward you?

_____

What can you be certain of, in regard to God's thoughts about you? Find the answer in Jeremiah 29:11.

_____

Looking back over this session, what is the most important discovery you have made about God's nature?

_____

RESPOND

Knowing about God is not enough—the way to spiritually grow is by living what you learn. In practical terms, how will you live out what you know about God's nature in your personal relationship with Him?

Because God is my Father, I will _____

Because God is my Lord and Savior, I will _____

Because God is my Teacher and Helper, I will _____

SCRIPTURE MEMORY

"My thoughts are nothing like your thoughts," says the LORD. "And my ways are far beyond anything you could imagine. For just as the heavens are higher than the earth, so my ways are higher than your ways and my thoughts higher than your thoughts."
—Isaiah 55:8–9

God is Three in One
A Biblical Sketch of God's Nature

GOD IS...	FATHER	SON	HOLY SPIRIT
ETERNAL	Psalm 90:2	Revelation 1:8; Colossians 1:15, 17; John 1:2	Hebrews 9:14
CREATOR	Isaiah 64:8; 1 Corinthians 8:6	John 1:3–4; Colossians 1:16–17	Genesis 1:1–2; Job 26:13; Job 33:4
TRUTH	2 Samuel 7:28; Isaiah 65:16	John 14:6	John 16:13

Developing Your Personal Quiet Time

Have you ever noticed how glued we are to our cell phones? When you stand in line now at the store, it seems like nobody talks to anyone anymore. Everyone just stares at their cell phones. People walk across busy intersections looking at their phone, heedless of the danger. And if you happen to leave home without your cell phone, you make sure to go back home and get it. It's almost a feeling of terror, isn't it?

But how much more should Christians be looking in God's Word! In fact, we should be longing for Scripture the same way we hunger for a meal. Job said, "I have not departed from his commands, but have treasured his words more than daily food" (Job 23:12).

Your pastor may serve up an excellent "meal" every Sunday, but if that's the only time you feed on God's Word, you're going to get very hungry.

You can take the basic Bible study skills you have used in this handbook and develop them for your own personal Bible reading. So let's review the three basic steps of Bible study.

READ the passage and pray for eyes to see. As the psalmist said, "Open my eyes to see the wonderful truths in your instructions" (Psalm 119:18).

Here are some questions to ask as you read:

- Who are the people in this passage? Who is speaking? What is happening? What is the main topic? What is the context?

REFLECT on what you have read. Pray for understanding. The Bible says, "Cause me to understand the way of your precepts, that I may meditate on your wonderful deeds" (Psalm 119:27 NIV).

Take time to consider what this passage teaches you about God, about life, and about yourself. Here are some questions to ask as you reflect:

- Is there a command to obey? Is there a promise to hold onto? Is there a condition to that promise? Is there a warning to heed? Is there an example to follow or avoid?

RESPOND to what you have learned. Pray for resolve to obey God's Word. The psalmist said, "I have considered my ways and have turned my steps to your statutes. I will hasten and not delay to obey your commands" (Psalm 119:59–60 NIV).

It's important to consider how the passage you have read might apply to your daily living. Here are some questions to ask yourself:

- Is there any sin mentioned that I need to confess? Does this point out any error in my actions or attitudes? What changes must I make? What can I do to follow the instructions or godly example given? How will I put this into practice in my life?

It will really help you to retain what you read if you write it down. Keep a notebook nearby to record what God has shown you. It might be exactly what you need for that day—or it may be a lesson that God wants to store in your heart for the future.

Finish your personal study time with prayer:

PRAISE and thank God for who He is and what He is doing.
REFLECT on what He has shown you. Repent of any known sin.
ASK God for help, strength, and guidance. Tell Him what you need!
YIELD to Him. Trust Him to work in your heart and in the events of your daily life.

At the end of this chapter, you will find some Bible passages to help you get started in your own personal study time.

Some Closing Thoughts

Now that you have completed *Start to Follow*, you should have a good understanding of the basic steps to spiritual growth. In some ways, you may feel like you've grown by leaps and bounds. In other ways, you may realize that you have only begun to scratch the surface. In every way, you can be certain that God will be faithful to complete the good work He has begun in you (see Philippians 1:6).

As you continue reading the Bible and applying it to your daily life, God will continue to transform your life and direct your steps. God bless you as you keep moving forward and growing in Him!

PERSONAL STUDY TIME

The Parable of the Good Samaritan
LUKE 10:30–37

READ

REFLECT

RESPOND

PRAYER

PERSONAL STUDY TIME

The Cure for Worry
MATTHEW 6:25–34

READ

REFLECT

RESPOND

PRAYER

PERSONAL STUDY TIME

What Is Love?
1 CORINTHIANS 13:4–7

READ

REFLECT

RESPOND

PRAYER

PERSONAL STUDY TIME

The Armor of God
EPHESIANS 6:10–17

READ

REFLECT

RESPOND

PRAYER

PERSONAL STUDY TIME

How to Be Blessed
PSALM 1:1–6

READ _____

REFLECT _____

RESPOND _____

PRAYER _____

Notes

Notes

Notes

Notes

APPLY TRUTH TO EVERYDAY LIFE

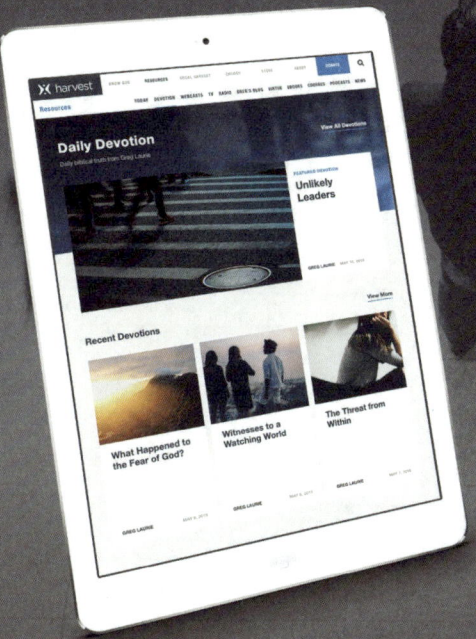

Receive daily emails full of encouragement, practical application, and biblical teaching from Pastor Greg Laurie.

SIGN UP AT
HARVEST.ORG/DEVOTIONS

TAKE A FREE ONLINE COURSE FROM HARVEST MINISTRIES.

As a new believer in Jesus Christ it is important that you get off on the right foot in your walk with Lord. Learning the essentials of what it takes to grow in this new relationship is key and Harvest wants to help you understand and implement these fundamental habits.

Harvest Ministries is committed to helping people know God and make Him known. That is why we have developed this free New Believer's Online Course, taught by Pastor Jonathan Laurie.

Through the practical, biblical principles taught in this four-session series, you will learn the importance of reading your Bible and praying daily, being an active member of the church, and sharing your faith.

This free online course is delivered by email, one lesson per week. Each week, you'll receive video teaching, reflection questions, and memory verses for deeper study.

You will come out of this four-week course with the tools you need to be successful in your new relationship with Jesus Christ.

Activate your free New Believer's Online Course, today!

courses.harvest.org/register/new-believers-course/